A Day with Doctors

by Jodie Shepherd

Content Consultant

Debra K. Gotz, M.D.

Reading Consultant

Jeanne Clidas, Ph.D.
Reading Specialist

Children's Press®
An Imprint of Scholastic Inc.
New York Toronto London Auckland Sydney
Mexico City New Delhi Hong Kong
Danbury, Connecticut

Library of Congress Cataloging-in-Publication Data
Shepherd, Jodie.
  A day with doctors / by Jodie Shepherd.
    p. cm. — (Rookie read-about community)
  Includes index.
  ISBN 978-0-531-28950-1 (library binding) — ISBN 978-0-531-29250-1 (pbk.)
  1. Medicine—Vocational guidance—Juvenile literature. 2. Physicians—Juvenile
literature. I. Title.
  R690.S48 2013
  610.69—dc23   2012013354

Produced by Spooky Cheetah Press

SCHOLASTIC, CHILDREN'S PRESS, ROOKIE READ-ABOUT®, and associated logos
are trademarks and/or registered trademarks of Scholastic Inc.

4 5 6 7 8 9 10 R 22 21 20 19 18 17 16 15 14

Photographs © 2013: iStockphoto: 15 (Blend Images), 28 (Damir Cudic); Media
Bakery: cover; PhotoEdit/Susan Van Etten: 11; Shutterstock, Inc./Monkey Business
Images: 19; Superstock, Inc./Science Faction: 16; Thinkstock: 20 (Brand X Pictures),
24 (Comstock), 8, 12 (Digital Vision), 23, 31 top left (Hemera), 3 top, 7, 31 bottom left
(iStockphoto), 4, 31 top right (Photodisc), 3 bottom, 27, 31 bottom right (Stockbyte).

Table of Contents

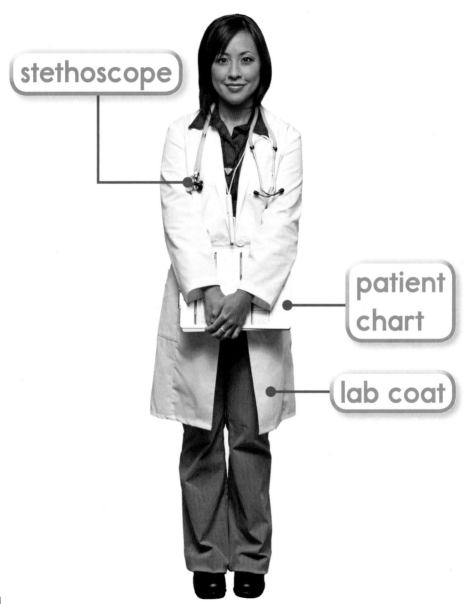

stethoscope

patient chart

lab coat

4

Meet a Doctor

Doctors take care of people.
They help keep us healthy.
Doctors also help people get
better when they are sick.

There are many kinds of doctors. Doctors who care for children are called pediatricians.

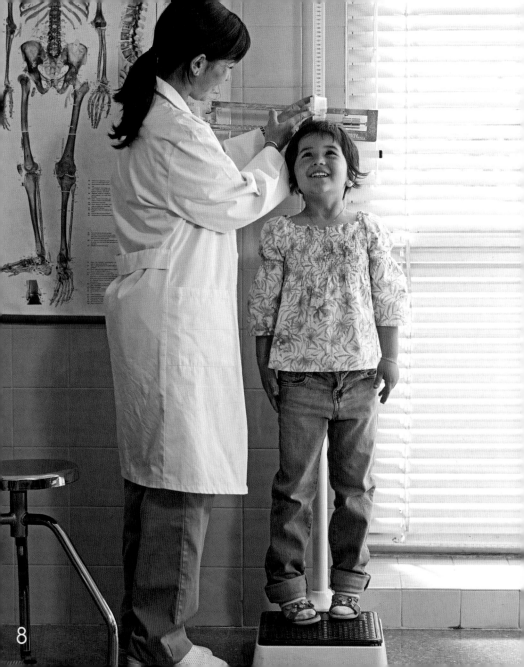

Checkup Time

Once a year, pediatricians see
healthy kids for a checkup.
The doctor wants to see how
much her patient has grown!

The doctor uses a stethoscope to listen to his patient's heart and lungs. He also takes her blood pressure.

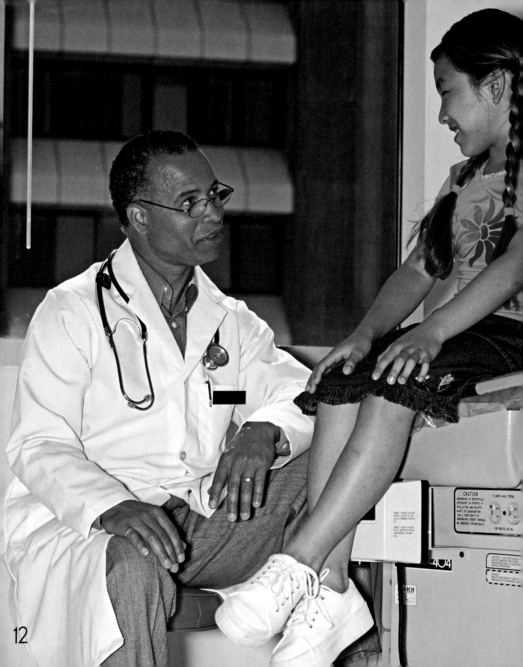

The doctor may also talk about how kids can feel their best. He might ask, "Do you eat healthy foods? Do you get plenty of sleep? Do you exercise?"

Sometimes doctors give shots. A shot helps keep people from getting sick. It pinches, but not for long.

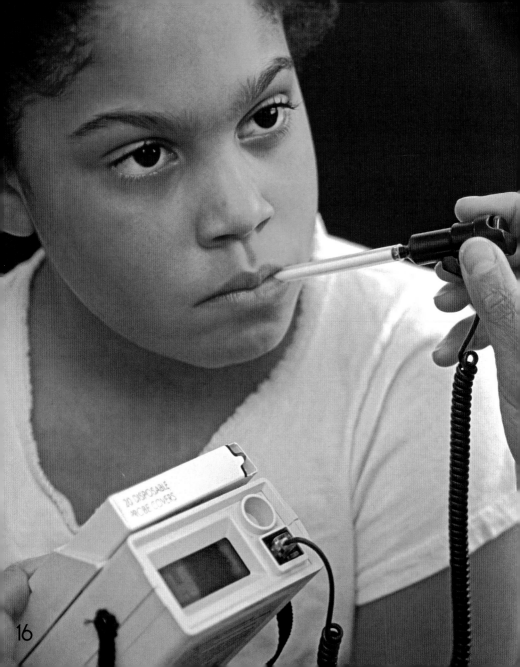

Here to Help!

Doctors also see people who are feeling sick. The doctor uses a thermometer to take the patient's temperature.

Say *aah!* The doctor uses a tongue depressor for a good look at the throat.

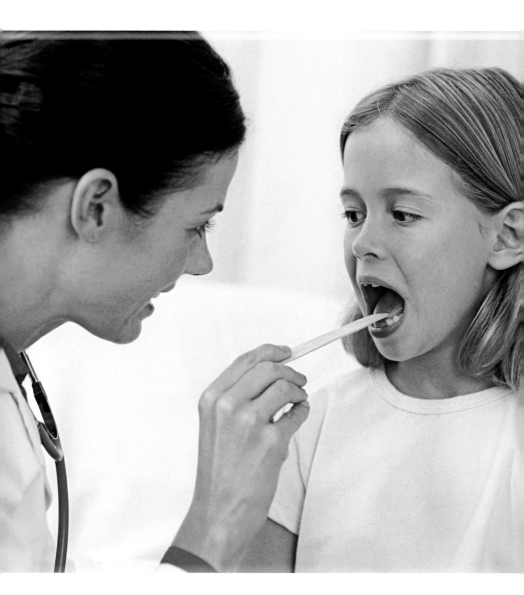

The doctor uses an otoscope to see into a child's ears.

Emergency!

Sometimes people have to go to the hospital. They might ride in an ambulance.

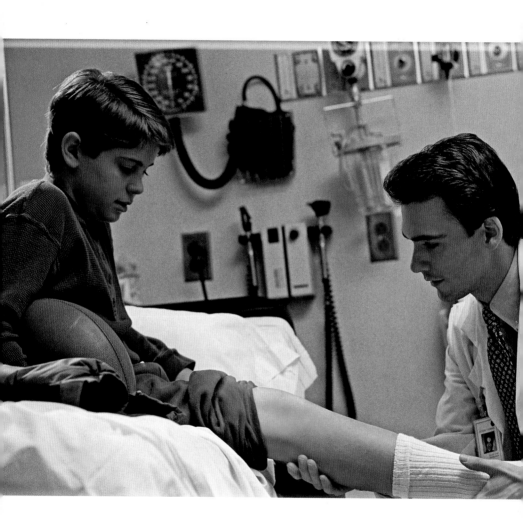

An emergency room doctor can help fix a broken bone or stitch a cut.

If a child needs an operation, she will go to a doctor who is a surgeon. The child will stay in the hospital until she is all better.

There are many different kinds of doctors. They do many different things. Doctors want to help you feel your best!

Try It! Look back at page 10. Can you check your heartbeat? Place your hand over your heart and feel it beat. Now dance for a minute or jump up and down. Feel your heartbeat again. Is it faster or slower than before you exercised?

Be a Community Helper!

- Stay healthy by eating good-for-you foods.

- Get lots of exercise to make your body strong.

- Make sure you get plenty of sleep.

- Wash your hands before you eat, after playing, and after you cough or sneeze.

- Remember to see your doctor once a year for a checkup!

Words You Know

ambulance

doctor

stethoscope

tongue
depressor

Index

Facts for Now

Visit this Scholastic Web site for more information on doctors:
www.factsfornow.scholastic.com
Enter the keyword **Doctors**

About the Author

Jodie Shepherd, who also writes under the name Leslie Kimmelman, is an award-winning author of dozens of books for children, both fiction and nonfiction. She is also a children's book editor.